SEARCH-AND-RESCUE
R O B O T S

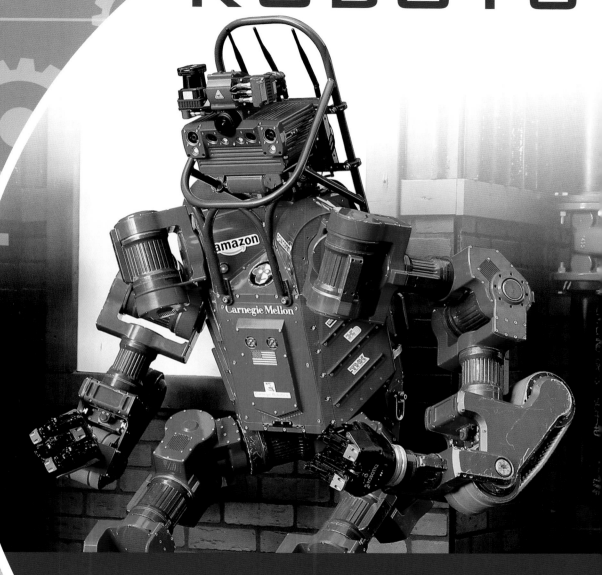

BY BRETT S. MARTIN

CONTENT CONSULTANT
David Hu
Associate Professor of Fluid Mechanics
Georgia Tech University

Core Library

An Imprint of Abdo Publishing
abdopublishing.com

Cover image: A robot designed for a disaster relief
robotics challenge stands ready to compete.

abdopublishing.com

Published by Abdo Publishing, a division of ABDO, PO Box 398166,
Minneapolis, Minnesota 55439. Copyright © 2019 by Abdo Consulting
Group, Inc. International copyrights reserved in all countries. No part of this
book may be reproduced in any form without written permission from the
publisher. Core Library™ is a trademark and logo of Abdo Publishing.

Printed in the United States of America, North Mankato, Minnesota
042018
092018

**THIS BOOK CONTAINS
RECYCLED MATERIALS**

Cover Photo: Chip Somodevilla/Getty Images News/Getty Images
Interior Photos: Chip Somodevilla/Getty Images News/Getty Images, 1; Pablo Ramos/AP Images,
4–5; Stefan Sauer/picture-alliance/dpa/AP Images, 9; Science & Society Picture Library/SSPL/
Getty Images, 12–13; Sam Ogden/Science Source, 16 (top); Kyodo/AP Images, 16 (middle top), 32,
38–39; Olivia Harris/Reuters/Newscom, 16 (middle bottom); Staff/Reuters/Newscom, 16 (bottom);
Visual China Group/Getty Images, 18–19; Kyodo/Newscom, 22; Klaus-Dietmar Gabbert/picture-
alliance/dpa/AP Images, 26–27; Alex Gallardo/AP Images, 29; Boris Roessler/picture-alliance/dpa/
AP Images, 31; Kiyoshi Ota/Getty Images News/Getty Images, 34–35

Editor: Bradley Cole
Imprint Designer: Maggie Villaume
Series Design Direction: Ryan Gale

Library of Congress Control Number: 2017962829

Publisher's Cataloging-in-Publication Data

Names: Martin, Brett S., author.
Title: Search-and-Rescue robots / by Brett S. Martin.
Description: Minneapolis, Minnesota : Abdo Publishing, 2019. | Series: Robot innovations |
        Includes online resources and index.
Identifiers: ISBN 9781532114700 (lib.bdg.) | ISBN 9781532154539 (ebook)
Subjects: LCSH: Robots in search and rescue operations--Juvenile literature. | Rescue
        work--Juvenile literature. | Search and rescue operations--Equipment and supplies--
        Juvenile literature. | Robots--Juvenile literature.
Classification: DDC 363.34--dc23

CONTENTS

INCREDIBLE SEARCH-AND-RESCUE ROBOTS

A severe earthquake shakes the city. It lasts less than one minute. That's enough to cause buildings to fall down. Sirens blare. Emergency vehicles flood the streets. First responders arrive at a collapsed building. People are stuck inside, so time is critical. Lives are at stake. Rescue workers are extremely careful, because the crumbled building is unstable.

Small robots climb over the rubble and fly overhead. Some slither through openings to

First responders search for survivors after an earthquake.

get inside the debris. What looks like a toy tank stops on a pile of concrete. It shines two lights and looks with a camera. Thirty feet (9 m) away, an operator moves a controller and watches her laptop. The tanklike robot, called a variable geometry tracked vehicle (VGTV), quickly responds. The track along its bottom shifts from flat to vertical. This raises the robot so it can peer inside an opening.

The robot's camera sends images to the laptop. The operator sees a person trapped inside. She calls for rescuers and shows

DESIGNING ROBOTS

STAND UP

VGTVs are small robots used for inspection. They can lift themselves up. The robots move on plastic tracks that change position. The tracks move from lying flat to standing up. This lets the robots increase in height. One model can go from 6 inches (15 cm) to 13.5 inches (34 cm) tall. By changing position, the robot can be small enough to get into tight spots but also can have the clearance to see over obstacles. This design feature is key to the VGTV's mission. VGTVs also can travel underwater.

them the location. It takes an hour, but the person is rescued.

In disasters, robots can go into situations too dangerous for humans. Robots provide search-and-rescue assistance on the ground, in the air, and in the water. Rescue robots can help save lives.

MANY TYPES OF DISASTERS, MANY TYPES OF ROBOTS

Search and rescue is an operation by emergency services crews. It can include trying to find someone who's lost, injured, or trapped. Hurricanes, mudslides, earthquakes, gas explosions, and terror attacks are disasters. They often cause a lot of damage. Those who are affected can be hard for search-and-rescue teams to reach. That's where robots play a vital role.

A robot is a machine designed to execute tasks. Robots often work quickly and with precision. They function in tough, dangerous conditions. They can work faster and move heavier loads than humans can.

They usually are operated by a human with a remote control. There are as many types of robots as there are jobs for them to do. They have been designed to help with all kinds of disasters. But the primary use of search-and-rescue robots is to find people.

Rescuers can send robots into a burning building to look for people. Robots can fly over an avalanche site. This lets rescuers see if anyone is stranded on the mountain. This is why responders say robots make "the invisible visible."

BETTER DESIGNS ENABLE MORE TASKS

Some of the first search-and-rescue robots were clumsy. They lost their balance as their weight shifted. This caused them to fall. Now, robots such as the Minitaur from Ghost Robotics can climb over rocks. It can also run and jump. Newer robots have overcome another earlier problem. Previously, they couldn't perform simple tasks, such as opening a door. Today's robots can open doors, turn valves, or connect hoses. They can use tools and climb ladders. These tasks can be needed to rescue people.

A rescuecopter can drop flotation devices to help save people in the water.

Some search-and-rescue robots are small so they can fit in tiny spaces. They can enter rubble piles to find people trapped underneath. Flying robots, or drones, can provide surveillance or fly over long distances.

This is important when debris prevents access to a disaster site. Drones have cameras. They help rescuers see damage and identify people in need of help.

Robots can also provide aid. Drones can drop lifesaving supplies to people before rescuers can reach them. The supplies can be food, water, or medicine. Other robots can deliver food to people stuck in a building to help them survive until they can be freed.

Rescuers can send robots into a collapsing building to look for people. Some robots have arms to move rubble and find survivors. Others can withstand radiation or are waterproof. These new advances help search-and-rescue robots find and help people.

STRAIGHT TO THE
SOURCE

Back in 2013, technology specialists had different opinions on what search-and-rescue robots could do. After the Robotics Challenge at the Defense Advanced Research Projects Agency (DARPA), one writer stated:

> Robots are generally still too limited in what they can do. They may be great for carrying out repetitive tasks in clutter-free environments, but entering a rubble-strewn building, climbing ladders, using fire hoses—these operations are beyond today's best robots. . . . But a robot that can do all that while operating in a deteriorated environment with limited access to communication and power, as DARPA is aiming for, is unheard of. That goal could easily take a decade or two.

> Source: Erico Guizzo. "DARPA's Rescue-Robot Showdown." *IEEE Spectrum*. IEEE, December 31, 2013. Web. Accessed October 20, 2017.

Point of View

The writer believes that robots are not ready for certain roles. According to him, what is it that makes robots not capable of helping in search-and-rescue missions? Are there other ways robots can help today? Think about the information in this book. Do you agree with the writer? Why or why not?

A SHORT BUT IMPACTFUL HISTORY

The term *robot* was created in 1920 by Karel Čapek. He was a Czechoslovakian writer. Čapek coined the word for his play, *Rossum's Universal Robots*. It comes from the word *rabota*, which means "forced labor." Robots are made to work in factories. Eventually, they fight back. Then they take over the world.

In real life, the first useful robots were not so dangerous. Robotic arms started working in factories in 1961. Engineers could program them for certain motions and tasks.

The Unimate robotic arm was the first robotic arm to work in a factory.

ROBOTS RESPONDING AROUND THE GLOBE

The Center for Robot-Assisted Search and Rescue (CRASAR) at Texas A&M University is dedicated to helping with disaster recovery. It does this with robots. The center has a program called Roboticists Without Borders. Its purpose is to provide robots in disasters worldwide. The program hopes to show the value of robots in search-and-rescue missions.

These robots helped build cars. Robots improved with technology.

THE DAWN OF SEARCH-AND-RESCUE ROBOTS

In 1979, a nuclear power plant in Three Mile Island in Pennsylvania had a severe accident. The power plant's reactor overheated. Dangerous gases were released. Luckily, no one was hurt. It was the worst nuclear accident in US history.

This led to the first use of robots helping with a disaster. In the 1980s, engineers at Carnegie Mellon University built robots to make repairs inside the damaged reactor.

On September 11, 2001, terrorists flew airplanes into the two World Trade Center towers in New York City. The buildings soon collapsed. Robots called Packbots were brought in to help.

The robots were approximately the size of a shoebox and had crane arms. They looked for survivors in the rubble. They also provided images that let engineers determine if an area was safe to send human rescuers. Robots have been used in search and rescue ever since.

DESIGNING ROBOTS

SENSORS CONTROL LEG MOVEMENTS

In search and rescue, robots encounter various surfaces. They might have to travel over anything from concrete or grass to mud or sand. The Minitaur from Ghost Robotics is designed to adapt to any terrain. The small, lightweight robot has sensors in its feet. The sensors feel the ground, then tell the robot how to react. The robot can then quickly change how fast it moves its legs. This lets the robot move at the fastest, safest speed for the conditions.

SERVING IN RECENT
DISASTERS

Today's search-and-rescue robots proved themselves in disasters:

September 2001

Terrorists attacked New York City. Robots searched for survivors.

March 2011

Robots measured radiation levels and fought fires after a nuclear accident in Fukushima, Japan.

April 2015

After an earthquake in Nepal, robots took pictures of roads and buildings to help organize recovery efforts.

September 2017

Robots helped inspect critical structures after hurricanes Harvey and Irma.

Examine the drones above. Which feature of each robot makes it well-suited for that disaster? Provide an argument to support your point.

During Hurricane Harvey, drones flew over Houston, Texas, for surveillance missions. Drone teams checked for downed trees and power lines. They also helped find clear routes for rescue workers. Teams flew drones around important structures such as bridges and sewer treatment stations to check for damage.

The Center for Robot-Assisted Search and Rescue (CRASAR) is from Texas A&M University. It flew 119 missions over Houston to help with recovery efforts. It sent drones to help with Hurricane Irma relief in Florida during September 2017 as well.

FURTHER EVIDENCE

Chapter Two talked about the history of robots. Check out the timeline at the website below. What are some developments that have helped search-and-rescue robots? What evidence is included to support this point? Does the information on the website support the main point of the chapter? Does it present new evidence?

WHAT TYPES OF SENSORS ARE USED IN ROBOTS?
abdocorelibrary.com/search-and-rescue-robots

陕西消防
SHANXI FIRE-FIGHTING

119

6

DESIGNING A ROBOT RESCUER

There are many types of disasters. Each one creates its own unique challenges. For example, rescuing people in a wildfire is different from helping people trapped inside a building. These are different still from human-made disasters, such as a bombing or nuclear accident. Designers and engineers make robots to handle each type of situation.

HIGH-TECH ABILITIES

A robot approaches a pile of debris. It uses a variety of high-tech sensors to help locate people. For instance, infrared sensors can find

Firefighting robots could one day help find survivors and fight fires alongside human firefighters.

people by their body heat. This allows rescuers to find survivors at night. A carbon-dioxide sensor can detect human breath. Listening sensors can even identify a person's heartbeat. Sensors can also identify odors, such as poisonous gas. Wi-Fi antennas and other attachments can detect signals. This locates people who are lost by zeroing in on mobile phones in the debris.

To reach victims, robots often need to climb over rubble without tumbling over. Robots are designed to perform their jobs on rough or uneven surfaces without falling. This is one of the most

ROBOT CHALLENGE

New robot technology is often put on display at competitions. The 2015 Defense Advanced Research Projects Agency (DARPA) Robotics Challenge offered $2 million in prize money. The goal was to discover the next generation of search-and-rescue robots. Twenty-four teams from around the globe competed in a type of robot Olympics. Robots had to perform certain tasks, such as driving a car and then getting out of it. The team that completed the most tasks the fastest won the prize money.

difficult things for rescue robots. Debris in disaster areas is often complex. So designers make robots that crawl, climb, slither, or fly. Having their weight mostly in their centers helps keep them balanced. Making robots that fly is the easiest way to overcome this obstacle.

ESSENTIAL SEARCH-AND-RESCUE FUNCTIONS

Reconnaissance and mapping are important tasks in search-and-rescue situations. Some missions make it hard for cameras to see. Cameras are especially useful when a disaster covers a wide area. An assessment of the crisis is often needed. This is where robots are currently the most useful. Drones and other robots can scan areas quickly. This provides essential information to rescuers.

Rescue teams need maps to know where to search. Robots provide information that can be used to create maps. They use different range finders and cameras to create maps of disaster areas. They even help generate

A team trains to use a drone for emergency situations.

three-dimensional maps. The maps can be used in wildfires, avalanches, and even at sea or underwater.

DESIGNING FRIENDLY, EFFICIENT ROBOTS

Rescue robots must be easy for humans to control. If not, giving commands might take too long or might not work properly. Every second matters when searching for disaster survivors. To make this process easier, some robots can take voice commands. The person can speak out loud to tell the robot what to do. Currently, some robots are hard to use and require lots of training. This is something that designers hope to fix in the future.

Other new technologies help robots look and act less robotic and more human. When people are trapped or lost, they are usually scared. When a robot shows up, it can scare the person even more. That's because robots can look frightening, especially when a person is already scared. Designers are trying to make robots less "creepy." They have robots play music, show videos, and let the survivor talk to human responders.

At a crisis site, robots should be able to go to work quickly. They should follow commands, even from a long distance. This usually means robots need to operate with remote controls. Being attached to a computer by a cord is a drawback. The cord can get caught on

DESIGNING ROBOTS

DESIGNED FOR MINES

Robots are sometimes designed to help in specific disasters. The Gemini-Scout Mine Rescue Robot by Sandia National Laboratories helps find people trapped in mining accidents. The robot can deliver food and supplies. Using tracks to move, Gemini-Scout can go over rubble, water, mud, and railroad tracks. Sandia engineer Justin Garretson said, "We focused a lot on usability and copied a lot of gamer interfaces so that users can pick it up pretty quickly." It uses an Xbox 360 controller and game interfaces to help workers use it quickly.

or cut by debris. A cord limits how far the robot can travel. Plus, robots should have the ability to quickly move through any environment.

Search-and-rescue robots may get damaged during a mission. They should be designed so that workers can fix them at a disaster site. Then the robots can get back to work quickly.

STRAIGHT TO THE
SOURCE

People get scared when they're trapped after a disaster. Dr. Robin Murphy, a professor at Texas A&M University, says a robot named Survivor Buddy can comfort them. It plays music to calm survivors. It also has a TV to let responders talk with survivors and check on their condition:

> If we find you in a building collapse with a robot, you are 20, 40, or 60 feet [6.1, 12.2, or 18.3 m] in the rubble. It can take rescuers between four and 10 hours to extricate you. . . . So what are we going to do with you for those hours? . . . If medical rescuers drive a robot up to you and start examining you, you're going to be that much more distressed. We made the robot move slower, more like a person, that respects personal space.

Source: Brooke Conrad. "Texas A&M Professor Part of Initiative that Produced Search-and-Rescue Robot, Survivor Buddy." *The Eagle.* The Eagle, August 10, 2013. Web. Accessed October 31, 2017.

Consider Your Audience

What if you had a younger brother trapped after a tornado and waiting with Survivor Buddy? What would you say to him? What will happen when the robot arrives? What can he expect during the rescue?

VARIETY OF SHAPES, SIZES, AND DESIGNS

The design of a robot determines what it can or cannot do. Robots with grasping arms can open doors. Robots with wings can fly. Robots with tracks can drive over rough ground. Someday a robot may be able to help in multiple emergency situations, but for now, each robot is designed for its job. And there are as many designs as there are jobs for search-and-rescue robots.

A rescue robot is able to open a door with its mechanical arm at a robotics competition.

TWO LEGS ARE NOT ALWAYS ENOUGH

A robot is walking through sand. It takes a few steps, then tilts to its right side. It tries to take another step, but its leg buckles. The robot lands face-first in the sand. Fortunately, this didn't happen during a search-and-rescue operation. It happened during a test. It showed that humanoid robots, which are built with two legs like humans, are not always effective.

Bipedal, or two-legged, robots carry a lot of weight in the top half of their body. This makes them unstable, which is why they fall.

DESIGNING ROBOTS

SOLVING AN ENERGY PROBLEM

The smallest robots have little room for big batteries. A common problem with tiny robots is that they run out of power quickly. RoboBee was designed to overcome this issue by using static electricity. The RoboBee was designed at Harvard's Wyss Institute for Biologically Inspired Engineering. It uses the static to stick to surfaces. This lets it save energy so it can focus on providing video.

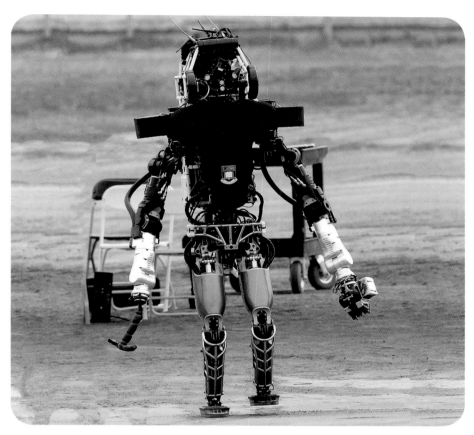

Standing on two legs, the Atlas performs in a DARPA challenge.

Robots with tracks like tanks or more than two legs are usually more stable. They sit lower to the ground, so there's less risk of tipping.

As bipedal robots benefit from better designs, they may become more useful in disasters. They could be able to run fast and perform jobs like humans.

This could include turning off valves that other robots can't reach.

PROVIDING EYES IN THE SKIES

Drones can help in another way. By flying high above an area, drones provide pictures or videos. This lets responders survey a large area. They can locate where people are stranded and need help.

Most drones used for search and rescue run on rechargeable batteries. They are flown by a remote control or a programmed computer inside the drone. Drones usually have radar, sensors, and cameras on board.

HELP ON THE GROUND

Unmanned ground vehicles, such as the VGTV, are called UGVs. They are used inside buildings or mines. In fact, one of their most common uses is for mine cave-ins. They often have tracks, like tanks, to help move over any surface. Some can even climb stairs. UGVs can have arms for moving items. Others just

A UGV meant to replace human rescue workers in dangerous situations in the future is shown off in Germany.

have cameras. UGVs sometimes have audio systems so rescuers can talk to victims.

Some UGVs are tiny. They look and move like insects or reptiles so they can enter small spaces. Others are big and brawny. They can move heavy pieces of rubble to clear the way for rescuers.

PARTS OF AN ROV

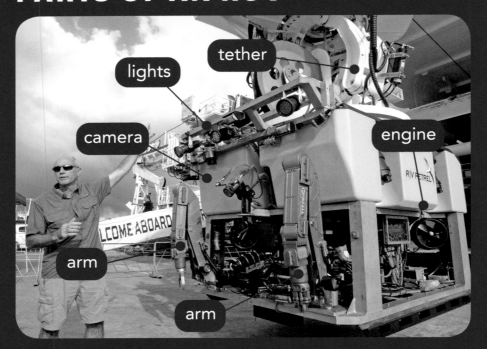

lights

tether

camera

engine

arm

arm

Can you identify the ROV's parts? How do these parts help it perform its mission? How would it perform search-and-rescue missions at sea?

TAKING TO THE WATER

A remotely operated vehicle, or ROV, is one type of unmanned underwater robot. These robots are used for bridge inspections after a hurricane or tsunami and for underwater recovery missions. ROVs often have video cameras, lights, sonar systems, and a moving arm. Unlike ground or air robots, ROVs are connected by a cable to a control device. Another type of underwater robot is the Unmanned Underwater Vehicles (UUVs). These robots do not have a tether and are made to operate under the water for longer.

ROVs are large. That's because ROVs need the power to move and steer underwater. They must be able to operate in rough waters. For example, four ROVs were used after an explosion on an oil rig in the Gulf of Mexico in 2010. The robots went into dangerous waters and dove deeper than humans could. They closed valves to keep oil from leaking into the ocean.

BREAKING THE ICE

Icebreakers are heavy, powerful ships that break through sea ice. They clear the way for other vessels. Russia wants to keep robots aboard its icebreakers. The robots would help in search-and-rescue missions. The ships operate in the Arctic region. The waters are freezing cold. Falling into the water can be deadly. Rescue robots could quickly rescue people who fall off the ship.

CHAPTER
FIVE

超音波検知装置(障害物等の検知)

THE FUTURE OF RESCUE ROBOTS

R obots could one day have a more involved role in search and rescue. Robots currently are limited in how they can help. But eventually, they may be able to take tasks from humans. They could cross debris better. They could start making more decisions on their own. They could also perform rescues themselves.

Currently, robots just provide information to search crews. The crews then rescue the victim. The Robo-Q is being designed to retrieve people. Sensors and cameras locate the person. Then an arm gently loads the

Robo-Q practices removing people from dangerous situations.

STUDYING RATTLESNAKES TO DESIGN A BETTER ROBOT

Rattlesnakes can shimmy up sand dunes without sliding back down. It's a feat few other snakes can do. Researchers want to see if robots can do the same thing. If robots could move like snakes, they could slither through piles of debris. However, previous snakelike robots had trouble moving through sand. By studying rattlesnakes, researchers learned that snakes move in a sideways motion. Their bodies moved horizontally up sandy hills. Scientists want robot snakes to mimic these same movements.

person onto a cart to be moved to safety. An early version of the robot is now being used. However, humans will always be needed. They have to program the robots and provide some guidance.

SNAKE- AND COCKROACH- INSPIRED ROBOTS

Engineers often look to animals for designs. That's how snakelike robots were created. Like snakes, these robots don't have legs, wheels, or tracks. That means the robots won't get stuck in holes or stopped by bumps in their path. Because snake robots are skinny, they can fit into narrow spaces.

Snakes aren't the only creepy creatures providing inspiration for robots. Designers also studied how fire ants move through confined spaces. Ants adjust the way they crawl based on the space they have to move around. They want to create robots that do the same.

Robots are also being based on cockroaches. Researchers at the University of California, Berkeley, designed a robot called CRAM. It stands for Compressible Robot with Articulated Mechanisms. It has an exoskeleton, like a cockroach. Just like the real bug, the robot is designed to crawl into tight spaces.

RELYING ON ARTIFICIAL INTELLIGENCE

When a city is hit by a tornado or earthquake or a forest fire is raging, communication can be hard. Power outages and damaged cell phone towers can

A robot designed to move like a snake can be fitted with a camera. Although it is still in development, it may help find survivors one day.

make mobile phones useless. Likewise, remote control signals to robots can be affected.

If a robot is sent into a dangerous situation and loses contact with its operator, the mission might stop.

One solution is to allow robots to think for themselves. This can be done with artificial intelligence (AI).

AI lets robots learn on their own, without a human telling them what to do. Robots can use AI to understand a situation, such as the loss of a radio signal.

DESIGNING ROBOTS

WALK-MAN COULD SAVE YOUR LIFE

Researchers in Italy are working on a humanoid robot that will do the job of human rescuers. The work at the Italian Institute of Technology has produced Walk-man. Software helps the robot balance and walk on two legs. Like a human, Walk-man has two arms, and both hands have four fingers and a thumb. This will help it perform jobs like humans do. The robot can drive a car. Approximately six feet (1.85 m) tall, the robot is designed to rescue victims. During testing, the robot will be taught to run into a burning building to find and rescue humans.

The robots can then decide what to do next. They might try to return to the place of the last signal. Or they may continue whatever they are doing until the signal is reconnected. Someday, AI may let robots work entirely on their own.

MORE ROBOTS COULD HELP SAVE MORE LIVES

Search-and-rescue robots will be used more often as more emergency response teams get them. When a team doesn't own a rescue robot, it can take days to borrow one. When a rescue unit does have a robot or a partnership with a group that does, a robot will arrive on the site much more quickly, even within hours. This is valuable time that teams can use to help rescuers.

EXPLORE ONLINE

Chapter Five discusses the future of search-and-rescue robots. The website below discusses how robots can use advanced technologies to do some tasks better than humans. What new information can you learn from this website?

SELF-LEARNING ROBOTS
abdocorelibrary.com/search-and-rescue-robots

FAST FACTS

- Robots are operated by a person using a remote control, computer, or other technology.

- There are many types of search-and-rescue robots, and they handle a variety of disasters.

- Robots have sensors and cameras to provide pictures, videos, and information. Sensors can identify people based on their body heat, heartbeat, or breath.

- Today, different designs let robots fly, crawl, or go underwater. The robots can go through harsh conditions, such as fires or explosions.

- Two-legged robots tip over easily. That's why search-and-rescue robots often have tracks or more than two legs.

- Companies are designing robots that look and act friendlier. This helps victims feel more comfortable when robots rescue them.

- Insects and snakes provide inspiration for robot designs.

- Advanced technologies such as AI allow robots to make some decisions on their own, without humans.

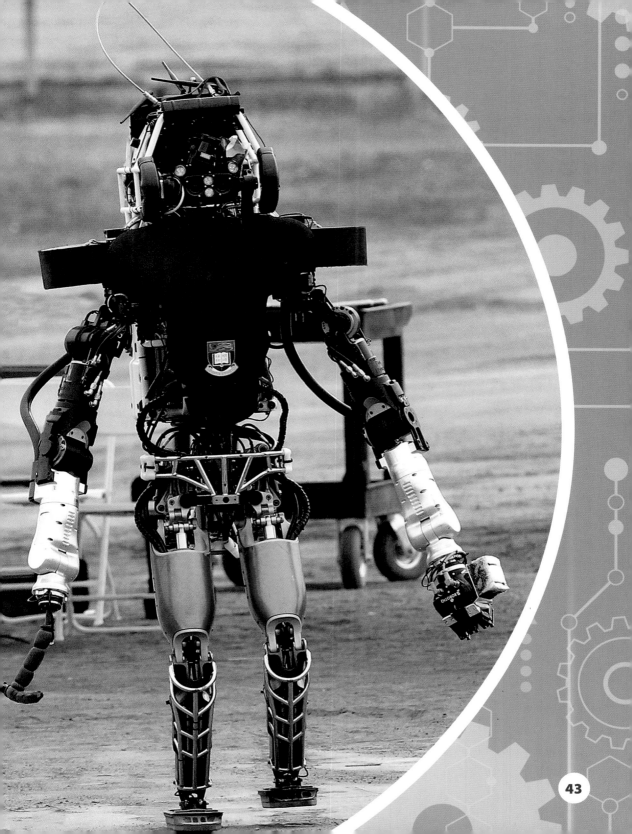

STOP AND
THINK

Say What?

Studying search-and-rescue robots can mean learning new words. Write five words or phrases in this book you've never heard before. Use a dictionary or the internet to find out what they mean. Then write the meanings in your own words. Use each word or phrase in a new sentence.

Another View

This book mentions artificial intelligence, which allows robots to make decisions without being told what to do by humans. Some people worry this will let robots learn on their own, and they will no longer need people to control them. Use the internet or library to find additional stories about artificial intelligence. Why is the technology controversial?

Take a Stand

Robots enter dangerous situations to save lives. Should taxpayer money be used to buy expensive robots for rescue teams? Do you think it's the best use of money for first responders? Are robots as important as other equipment?

You Are There

This book talks about drones. Imagine you are the pilot of a drone, flying it with a remote control. You have a computer screen that shows what the drone sees. You fly it over a wildfire. Write an email to your friends describing what you see. Include details on anything you see that's unexpected. How can you help rescue people trapped by the fire below?

GLOSSARY

artificial intelligence
the ability of robots or machines to learn on their own

assessment
the act of making a judgment or choosing between different things

drone
a flying robot that usually provides pictures or videos

high-tech
advanced technology that allows robots to perform complex tasks

humanoid
a robot that is designed to resemble a human and has two legs

program
a set of instructions for a robot given through a computer

reconnaissance
a mission to observe a region or activities

responder
a trained person, such as a firefighter, who responds to a disaster

surveillance
keeping a constant watch on people or an area

terrain
the features or type of surface for a piece of land

tsunami
a huge wave created by an underwater volcano or earthquake

ONLINE RESOURCES

To learn more about search-and-rescue robots, visit our free resource websites below.

Visit **abdocorelibrary.com** for free Common Core resources for teachers and students, including vetted activities, multimedia, and booklinks, for deeper subject comprehension.

Visit **abdobooklinks.com** for free additional online weblinks for further learning. These links are routinely monitored and updated to provide the most current information available.

LEARN MORE

Koontz, Robin. *Robotics in the Real World*. Minneapolis: Abdo Publishing, 2015.

Shulman, Mark. *TIME For Kids Explorers: Robots*. New York: Time For Kids, 2014.

INDEX

About the Author

Brett S. Martin has more than 20 years of writing experience. He has worked as a reporter, editor, director of public relations, and president of his own media company. He has written for more than two dozen magazines and has written several fiction and nonfiction books. Martin lives in Shakopee, Minnesota, with his wife and two teenage sons.